PIANO . VOCAL . GUITAR

ISBN 978-1-4950-4926-2

7777 W. BLUEMOUND RD. P.O. BOX 13819 MILWAUKEE, WI 53213

In Australia Contact:
Hal Leonard Australia Pty. Ltd.
4 Lentara Court
Cheltenham, Victoria, 3192 Australia
Email: ausadmin@halleonard.com.au

For all works contained herein:
Unauthorized copying, arranging, adapting, recording, Internet posting, public performance,
or other distribution of the printed music in this publication is an infringement of copyright.
Infringers are liable under the law.

Visit Hal Leonard Online at
www.halleonard.com

4	All She Wants Is
12	Come Undone
26	Electric Barbarella
18	Girls on Film
7	Hungry Like the Wolf
42	I Don't Want Your Love
48	Is There Something I Should Know
35	New Moon on Monday
62	Notorious
70	Ordinary World
55	Planet Earth
88	The Reflex
77	Rio
106	Save a Prayer
114	Serious
99	Skin Trade
124	Union of the Snake
130	A View to a Kill
135	The Wild Boys

ALL SHE WANTS IS

Words and Music by JOHN TAYLOR, NICK RHODES and SIMON LeBON

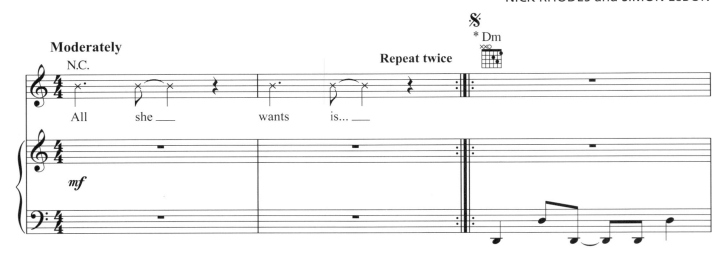

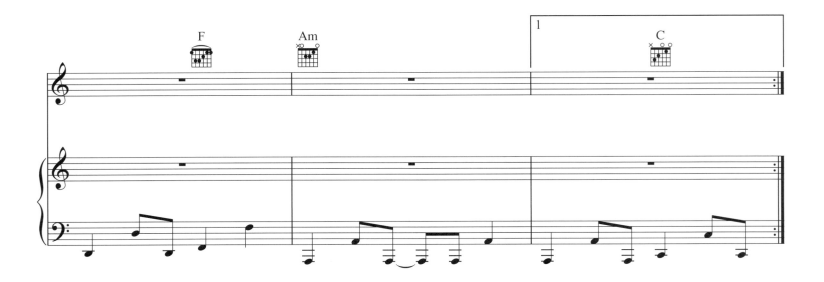

*Chord symbols reflect implied harmony.

Copyright © 1988 Skintrade Music, Ltd.
All Rights Administered by Songs Of SMP
All Rights Reserved Used by Permission

COME UNDONE

Words and Music by JOHN TAYLOR,
NICK RHODES, SIMON LeBON
and WARREN CUCCURULLO

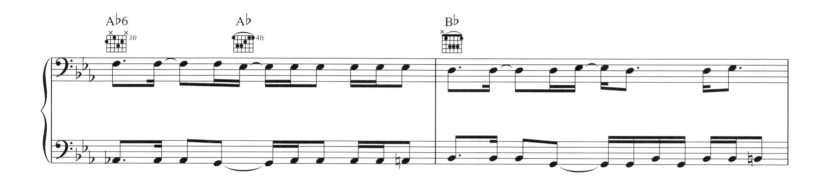
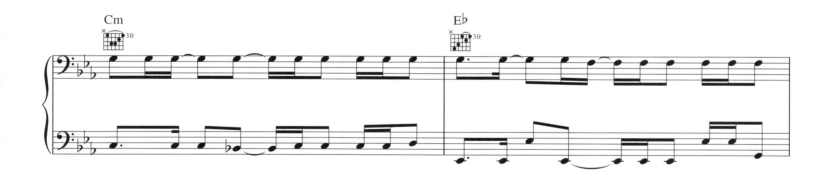

Copyright © 1993 Skintrade Music, Ltd. and Private Parts Music
All Rights for Skintrade Music, Ltd. Administered by Songs Of SMP
All Rights for Private Parts Music Administered by BMG Rights Management (US) LLC
All Rights Reserved   Used by Permission

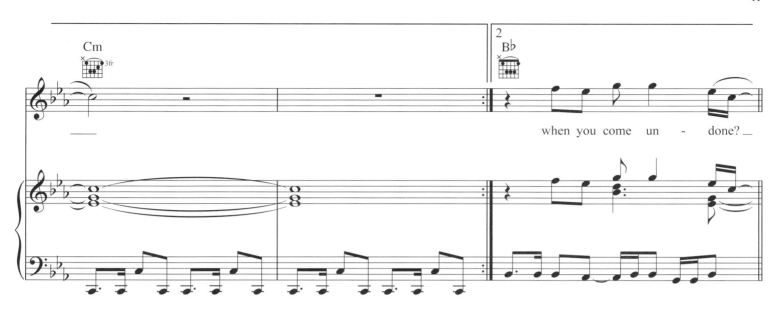

GIRLS ON FILM

Words and Music by JOHN TAYLOR, ANDY TAYLOR, NICK RHODES, ROGER TAYLOR and SIMON LeBON

Copyright © 1981 Gloucester Place Music Ltd.
All Rights Administered by Sony/ATV Music Publishing LLC, 424 Church Street, Suite 1200, Nashville, TN 37219
International Copyright Secured All Rights Reserved

ELECTRIC BARBARELLA

Words and Music by NICK RHODES, SIMON LeBON and WARREN CUCCURULLO

I DON'T WANT YOUR LOVE

Words and Music by JOHN TAYLOR,
NICK RHODES and SIMON LeBON

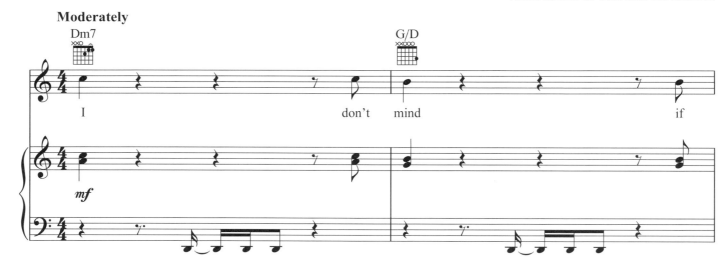
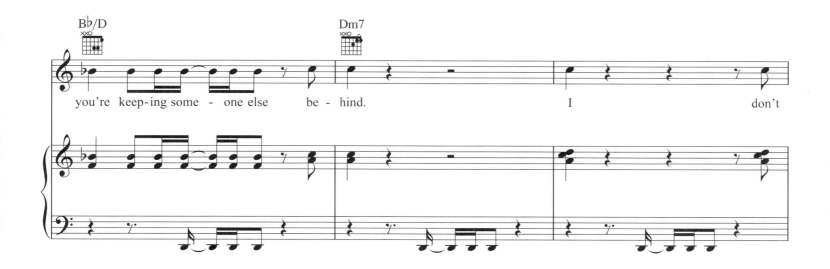

Copyright © 1988 Skintrade Music, Ltd.
All Rights Administered by Songs Of SMP
All Rights Reserved   Used by Permission

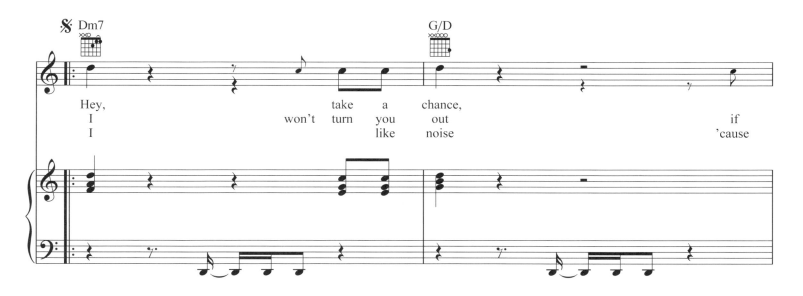
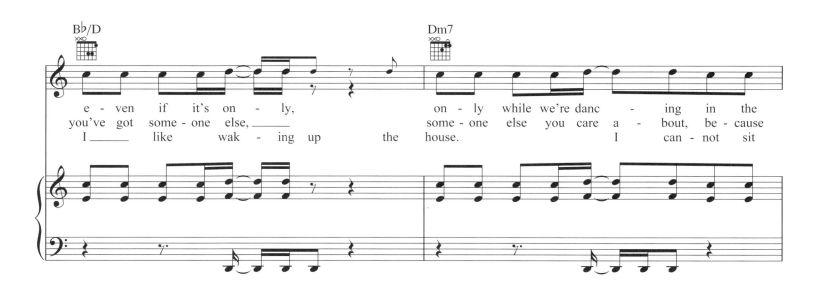
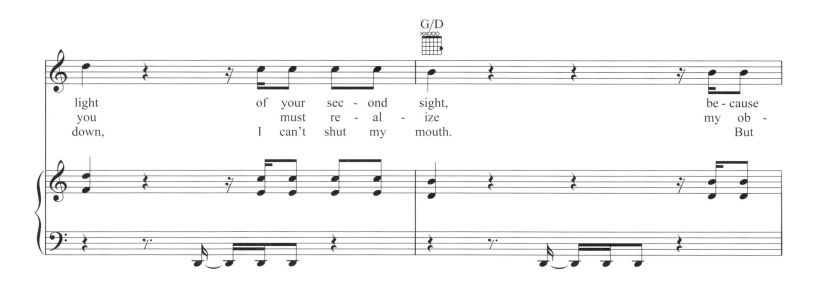

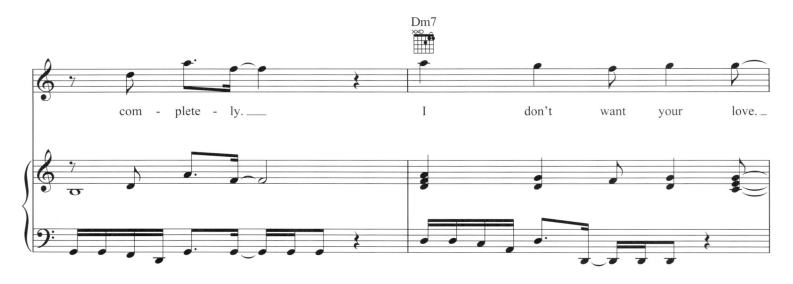

Is There Something I Should Know

Words and Music by JOHN TAYLOR, ANDY TAYLOR, NICK RHODES, ROGER TAYLOR and SIMON LeBON

PLANET EARTH

Words and Music by JOHN TAYLOR, ANDY TAYLOR, NICK RHODES, ROGER TAYLOR and SIMON LeBON

Copyright © 1981 Gloucester Place Music Ltd.
All Rights Administered by Sony/ATV Music Publishing LLC, 424 Church Street, Suite 1200, Nashville, TN 37219
International Copyright Secured   All Rights Reserved

NOTORIOUS

Words and Music by JOHN TAYLOR,
NICK RHODES and SIMON LeBON

Copyright © 1993 Skintrade Music, Ltd.
All Rights Administered by Songs Of SMP
All Rights Reserved   Used by Permission

ORDINARY WORLD

Words and Music by JOHN TAYLOR,
NICK RHODES, SIMON LeBON
and WARREN CUCCURULLO

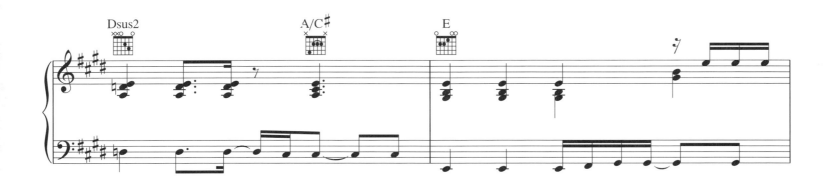

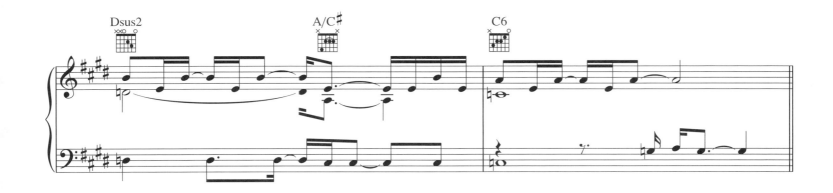

Copyright © 1993 Skintrade Music, Ltd. and Private Parts Music
All Rights for Skintrade Music, Ltd. Administered by Songs Of SMP
All Rights for Private Parts Music Administered by BMG Rights Management (US) LLC
All Rights Reserved   Used by Permission

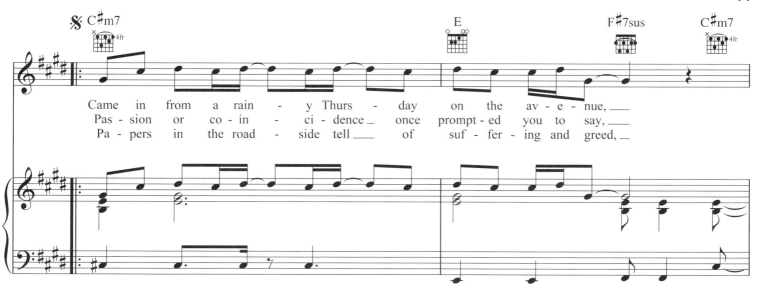

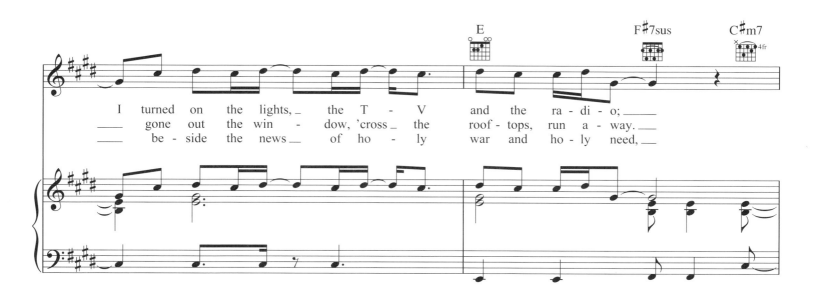

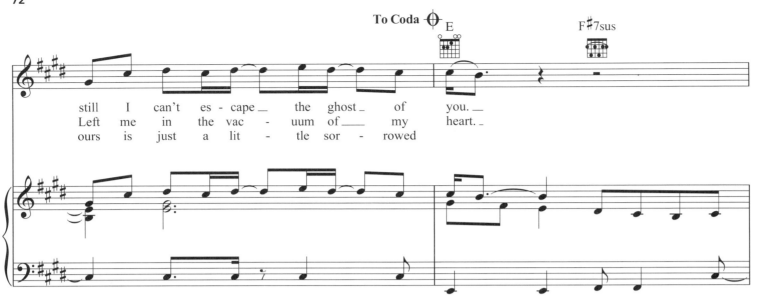

RIO

Words and Music by JOHN TAYLOR, ANDY TAYLOR, NICK RHODES, ROGER TAYLOR and SIMON LeBON

Copyright © 1982 Gloucester Place Music Ltd.
All Rights Administered by Sony/ATV Music Publishing LLC, 424 Church Street, Suite 1200, Nashville, TN 37219
International Copyright Secured   All Rights Reserved

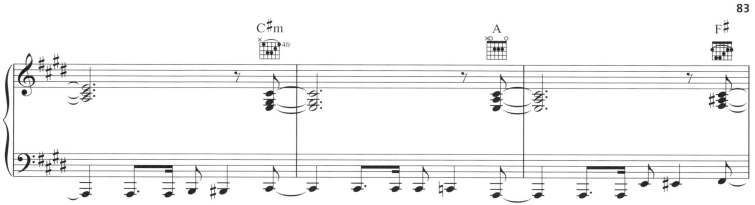

Saxophone solo ad lib.

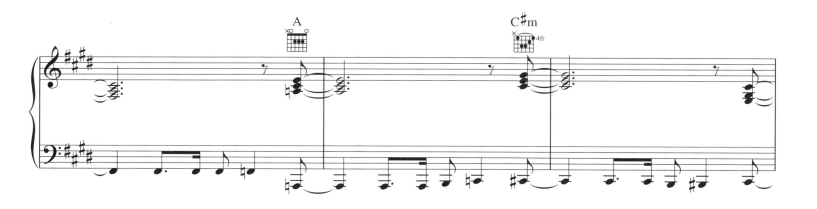
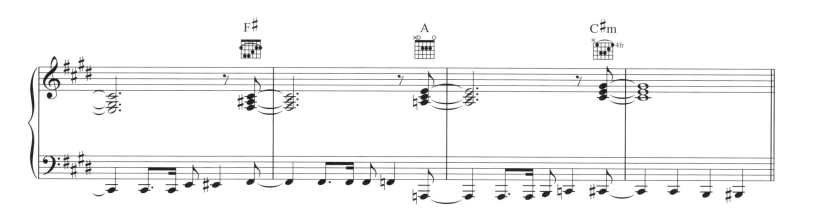

THE REFLEX

Words and Music by ANDY TAYLOR,
JOHN TAYLOR, NICK RHODES,
ROGER TAYLOR and SIMON LeBON

8vb throughout

Copyright © 1983 Actionlink Ltd., Gloucester Place Music Ltd., Hintcrest Ltd., Youngstown Ltd. and Noticevale Ltd.
All Rights Administered by Sony/ATV Music Publishing LLC, 424 Church Street, Suite 1200, Nashville, TN 37219
International Copyright Secured All Rights Reserved

treas - ure in ___ the dark ___ and watch - ing o - ver luck -

- y clo - ver. Is - n't that __ bi - zarre? ___ And

ev - 'ry lit - tle thing the re - flex does __ {leaves you an - swered / is an an - swer} with a ques - tion mark. __

SKIN TRADE

Words and Music by JOHN TAYLOR,
NICK RHODES and SIMON LeBON

Working on the week-end, ba-by, she's work-ing all through the night.
Doc-tors of the rev-o-lu-tion gave us the med-i-cine we de-sired.

A jump in-to the deep end gave her the
Be-sides be-ing ab-so-lute-ly pain-less, it's a

Copyright © 1993 Skintrade Music, Ltd.
All Rights Administered by Songs Of SMP
All Rights Reserved   Used by Permission

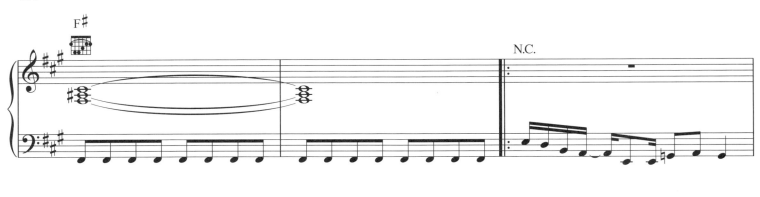

110

SERIOUS

Words and Music by SIMON LeBON,
NICK RHODES, JOHN TAYLOR,
STERLING CAMPBELL and WARREN CUCCURULLO

Copyright © 1990 Simon LeBon Publishing, Nick Rhodes Publishing, John Taylor Publishing, Sterling Campbell Publishing and Private Parts Music
All Rights for Private Parts Music Administered by BMG Rights Management (US) LLC
All Rights Reserved   Used by Permission

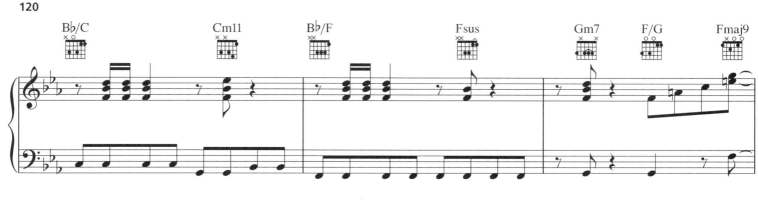

UNION OF THE SNAKE

Words and Music by ANDY TAYLOR,
JOHN TAYLOR, NICK RHODES,
ROGER TAYLOR and SIMON LeBON

Copyright © 1983 Actionlink Ltd., Gloucester Place Music Ltd., Hintcrest Ltd., Youngstown Ltd. and Noticevale Ltd.
All Rights Administered by Sony/ATV Music Publishing LLC, 424 Church Street, Suite 1200, Nashville, TN 37219
International Copyright Secured All Rights Reserved

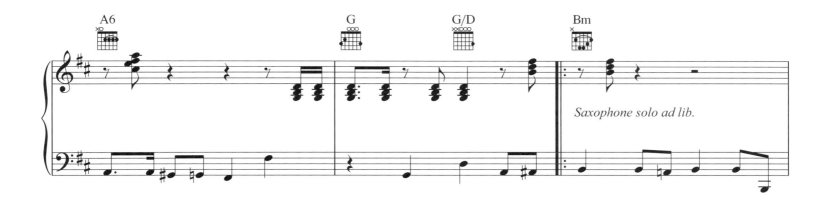
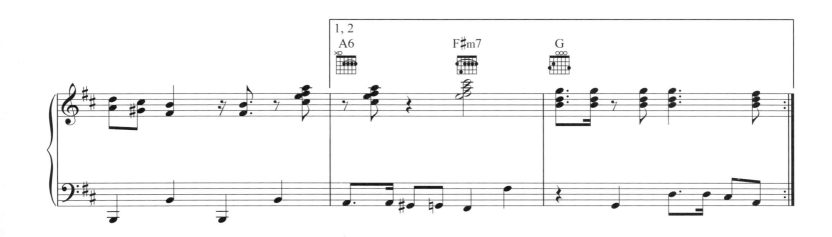

A VIEW TO KILL

Words and Music by JOHN TAYLOR,
ANDY TAYLOR, NICK RHODES,
JOHN BARRY, SIMON LeBON
and ROGER TAYLOR

Additional Lyrics

2. Choice for you is the view to a kill.
   Between the shades, assassination standing still.
   The first crystal tears
   Fall as snowflakes on your body.
   First time in years,
   To drench your skin with lovers' rosy stain.
   A chance to find a phoenix for the flame,
   A chance to die, but can we...
   Chorus

THE WILD BOYS

Words and Music by ANDY TAYLOR,
JOHN TAYLOR, NICK RHODES,
ROGER TAYLOR and SIMON LeBON

Moderately

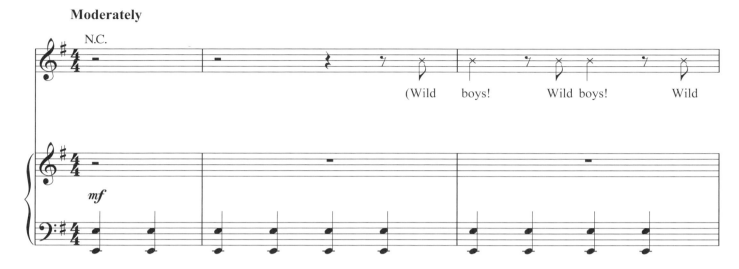

(Wild boys! Wild boys! Wild

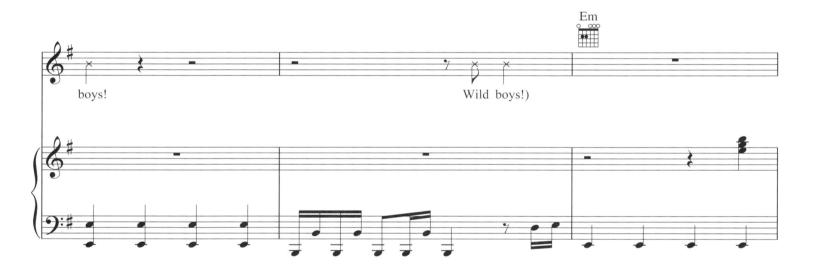

boys! Wild boys!)

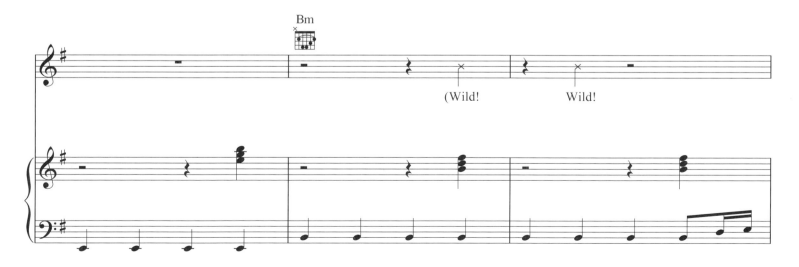

(Wild! Wild!

Copyright © 1983 Actionlink Ltd., Gloucester Place Music Ltd., Hintcrest Ltd., Youngstown Ltd. and Noticevale Ltd.
All Rights Administered by Sony/ATV Music Publishing LLC, 424 Church Street, Suite 1200, Nashville, TN 37219
International Copyright Secured All Rights Reserved